ADVICE FROM 1 DISCIPLE OF MARX
TO 1 HEIDEGGER FANATIC

ADVICE FROM 1 DISCIPLE OF MARX

TRANSLATED BY COLE HEINOWITZ
AND ALEXIS GRAMAN

TO 1 HEIDEGGER FANATIC

MARIO SANTIAGO PAPASQUIARO

WAVE BOOKS

SEATTLE AND

NEW YORK

Published by Wave Books   www.wavepoetry.com

Wave Books titles are distributed to the trade by Consortium Book Sales and Distribution
Phone: 800-283-3572 / SAN 631-760X

This title is available in a limited edition directly from the publisher

Library of Congress Cataloging-in-Publication Data
Santiago Papasquiaro, Mario
    [Jeta de Santo. English. Selections]
    Advice from 1 disciple of Marx to 1 Heidegger fanatic / Mario Santiago Papasquiaro ; translated by Cole Heinowitz and Alexis Graman.
        p. cm.
    "Originally published in Jeta de Santo (Antología Poética, 1974–1997) 2008, Fondo de Cultura Económica de España" —T.p. verso.
    ISBN 978-1-933517-68-1
    I. Heinowitz, Cole. II. Graman, Alexis. III. Title. IV. Title: Advice from one disciple of Marx to one Heidegger fanatic.
    PQ7298.29.A466A613 2013
    861'.7—dc23   2012025412

Designed and composed by Quemadura   Printed in the United States of America

9 8 7 6 5 4 3 2 1 FIRST EDITION

I don't think; I bite. —MARIO SANTIAGO PAPASQUIARO

M ost readers have never heard of José Alfredo Zendejas Pineda (1953–1998). A few might know him by his pseudonym, Mario Santiago Papasquiaro. But many readers know the lovably eccentric character he inspired, Ulises Lima, from Roberto Bolaño's *The Savage Detectives*: "a ticking bomb" who wrote incessantly "in the margins of books that he stole and on pieces of scrap paper that he was always losing," but who "never wrote poems." While there is certainly some truth to Bolaño's portrait of his friend, the real Santiago was extremely prolific, leaving behind over 1,500 manuscript pages at the time of his death.

In his early twenties, Santiago was the terror of Mexican literary society, interrupting readings to declaim his own poems, insulting the featured readers, and even starting brawls. In 1975, along with several friends (among them Bolaño), he founded the radical Infrarealist poetry movement. Santiago and the "Infras" drew on a wide range of sources, from Baudelaire, Rimbaud, and Lautréamont, to

Dadaism, Surrealism, Stridentism, and the Beats. Santiago was also influenced by the leftist, avant-garde Peruvian poetry movement Hora Zero and by Mexican writer-activists such as Efraín Huerta and José Revueltas (the pseudonym "Santiago Papasquiaro" comes from the town where Revueltas was born). For Santiago, poetry and politics were inseparable.

Frustrated by the rigidity of the Mexican literary world (and chasing the poet Claudia Kerik), Santiago left the country. He was a thief in Paris, a fisherman on the coast of France, a political prisoner in Vienna, an agricultural day laborer in Spain, and a kibbutznik in Israel. When he returned home at the end of the '70s, little had changed. Literary Mexico remained as institutionalized and conservative —and as utterly hostile to Santiago—as before. Experimenting with hallucinogens and meandering for hours through the mazes of Mexico City, Santiago continued to challenge aesthetic and cultural norms, insisting: "I'm only interested in poetry that springs from flaming labyrinths."

By the '90s, Santiago had drifted far from his old Infrarealist comrades. He would disappear for days, without warning, lost in the ghettos and on the outskirts of the city. In the course of his wanderings, he was hit by a car—twice. The first time left him bludgeoned and forced to walk with a cane. The second time was fatal.

"Advice from 1 Disciple of Marx to 1 Heidegger Fanatic" (1975) is considered by some as the canonical poem of Infrarealism. Built from the collision of "low" and "high" culture—of police brutality and drunken ranting with Modernism and German phenomenology—it is a testament of resistance to political and artistic repression comparable to Ginsberg's "Howl." In the Infrarealist manifesto Bolaño writes, "The true imagination is the one that dynamites, elucidates, injects emerald microbes into other imaginations. . . . Perception opens by way of an ethic-aesthetic taken to the extreme." No one embodied these ideas with the visceral ferocity of Santiago. Or as another fellow Infra put it: Bolaño "portrayed the bleeding heart," but only Santiago "held it in his hand."

COLE HEINOWITZ

ADVICE FROM 1 DISCIPLE OF MARX

TO 1
HEIDEGGER
FANATIC

it's as well at times

To be reminded that nothing is lovely,

Not even in poetry, which is not the case.

W. H. AUDEN

The world gives you itself in fragments / in splinters:

    in 1 melancholy face you glimpse 1 brushstroke by Dürer

    in someone happy the grimace of 1 amateur clown

    in 1 tree: the trembling of birds sucking from its crook

    in 1 flaming summer you catch bits of the universe licking its face

the moment 1 indescribable girl

    rips her Oaxacan blouse

just at the crescent of sweat from her armpits

& beyond the rind is the pulp / & like 1 strange gift of the eye

               the lash

Maybe not even Carbon 14 will be able to reconstruct the true facts

The days are gone when 1 naturalist painter

could ruminate over the excesses of lunch

between movements of Swedish gymnastics

& without losing sight of the rose-blue tones of flowers he wouldn't have imagined

    even in his sweetest nightmares

We are actors of infinite acts

      & not exactly under the blue tongue

            of movie spotlights

for example now / that you see how Antonioni passes by

                with his usual little camera

observed by those who prefer to bury their heads in the grass

to get drunk on smog or whatever / so as not to add

                          to the scandals

that already make the public roads impassable

by those who were born to be lavishly kissed by the sun

& its earthly ambassadors

by those who talk of fabulous copulations / of females you can't believe

               in this geological age

of vibrations that would make you 1 fervent propagandist for Zen Buddhism

by those who at 1 point were saved

from the accidents the crime rags call substantial

& that by the way—for now—aren't counted among the flowers of the Absurd

That's how it is on the trapeze on the tightrope

                    of this 1,000-ring circus

1 old man rattles on about the thrill he felt at seeing Gagarin

fluttering like 1 fly in outer space
& pity the starship wasn't called Icarus I
that Russia is so fiercely anti-Trotskyite
      & then his voice dissolves / collapses
         between cheers & boos

Reality & Desire get thrashed / get chopped up
they spill out over each other
like they never would in 1 of Cernuda's poems
foam runs from the mouth of the 1 who speaks wonders
& it would seem he lived in the clouds
      & not on the outskirts of this barrio

The humid air of April / the lewd wind of autumn /
      the hail of August & July
all here present with their fingerprints

Alcohol
piss / what hasn't fertilized this grass
how many sub-minimum-wage gardeners will leave their watery proteins
      in this trap

For now you stretch out face down toward the shade

                of the long & hairy legs of the parks

      where they gather:

the 1 who dreams of revolutions that stay too long in the Caribbean

the 1 who'd like to rip out the eyes of the billboard heroes

to expose the hollowness of the farce

the girl with the feline & filmic green eyes

even if on getting closer they turn out to be blue or who knows

the student all adrenaline & erupting pores

the 1 who believes in nobody / nor in the Kantian beauty

        of some admirers of Marcuse

& bursts out yelling that we're putrefied by rage /

dehydrated from so many tomes of theory

the occasional little whore who shares the torrent of her solitude

            with strangers

letting grace sympathy sudden vibrations tip the scale

      of supply & demand

Chance: that other antipoet & incorruptible bum

those who come here to weep / until they carve for themselves—as in wood—

        the face of some paranoid martyr

after smashing—not exactly from devotion—

          the seats of the movie theaters

the 1 who writes his will or his epitaph on 1 wrinkled napkin

& then blows kisses to the wind / —& everyone assumes

it's his birthday or last night he got hitched in holy matrimony—

& all the hypotheses turn out too fragile to explain

why he used 1 gun & not 1 can of paint

if he seemed capable of seducing to the point of fever / the pulse

                                        & the pupil of Giotto

the 1 who always greets you with *I'm desperate*

                        & yourself?

those who love rabidly like street dogs

            —through thick & thin—

& 1 calls them blooming lovers

& they're aphrodisiacs not only to the sensibilities of Marc Chagall

those who meet death in person

in the hour when suicide becomes an obsession

1 disheveled desire to bite & be bitten

to have done with all those pipe dreams

                                that seem indestructible

to momentarily create such a Power

that the daily cement mixers destroy you

            like 1 brown paper bag

& then you understand the 1 who'd like to bury

       under mountains of plants

        buildings / black earth

the slightest beat / the tachycardia of his intimate history

you're infected with the nervousness the anxiety

    of those who act like they breathe

like they have a certain trace of carnivorous plants about them

& spend hours waiting for their companion Tenderness

     that call girl who rarely arrives

those who come running from the tear gases

& billy clubs of the major avenues

of the major & minor stains that can't be removed

with Pine-Sol or 1 stroke of 1 Kleenex

those who ignore who they are / *& don't even want to know*

when the climate's reputation gets worse by the day

those perpetual sufferers from amnesia who suck their thumbs with joy

because the Earthly Paradise is here & not in Miami

those who promise to declare this autonomous territory independent island

that will not degrade into scrap metal ruins supermarkets

At the moment 1 hit song
                entangles its rhythm
with the rain's strange samba
& 1 fatally fleeting order is established
so they can continue to dominate the scene
                hair in disorder /
                        enormous eyes moist
& as if risen from the very chiaroscuro of the night
1 girl appears her muddy fists against her thighs
repeating 1 / 2 / 3 times:
I am not 1 sex object / I am not that you robots /
                I'm alive / like 1 forest of eucalyptus
here where the norm is to be implacably nice
                        to each other
                & this is the lesser evil

The park trembles / my inner steps carry me
through the streets of 1 green seaport
                the natives call *Mescaline*
        1 sensation unknown until now
like being scientifically certain what DNA tastes like
                after making love

If this isn't Art I'll slash my vocal cords
my tenderest testicle / I'll stop blathering
                  if this isn't Art

1 tree branch bends under the weight of 1 sparrow
or rather 1 sparrow ends up shattering 1 branch that's already broken

            We're still alive
somehow or other we must name the islands of crystals
that with the luxury of violence trample the softest regions of your eyes
reality seems like 1 miniature made to scale from mica
but also your eyelids your perception & its straitjacket
                                  Material & Energy /
& the courage to stick your tongue inside their tongue

This is 1 very peculiar day
vibrant quotidian anonymous
absolutely earthly as we often say on days of celebration
                  or during the ever more frequent house raids
the fear lights up your stomach & it burns

THERE IS NO AHISTORICAL ANGUISH

TO LIVE HERE IS TO HOLD YOUR BREATH

& UNDRESS

—Advice from 1 disciple of Marx to 1 Heidegger fanatic—

Poetry: we're still alive
         & you light my cheap cigar with your matches
             & you look at me like 1 insignificant mop-top
shivering with cold in the comb of the night

                   We're still alive

1 green-eyed & yellow-winged butterfly
         has pinned itself to my jacket's blue lapel
—my denim body
         feels seductive human radar pollen magnet
acquires at times the conviction of 1 miniature galaxy
         singing sheer absurdities between ohs of amazement—
Damn what a moon!

exclaims the millionaire in solitude

                             & miserable at work

who just yesterday was laid off for not getting excited

by the short-circuits of the bureaucratic coffeemaker

What a moon!

           like 1 clipped nail

                 like 1 glob of sperm

                    suspended

          over the bristling back of the night

when you hear

the crunch of smashed nuts—crack—

the whirring the whine of the ambulance

                 that once again arrives too late

the murmur of lizards with leopard spots

mischievously climbing through vines in search of food

the last sounds of 1 picnic

                 where Desolation has been at it again

& has finished by announcing the approach of the wind

                    that stains & corrodes everything

Nevertheless 1 still walks around here like 1 happy sparrow

like Chaplin the day he first kissed Mary Pickford

someone goes by with 1 transistor radio

                             that seems like his second ear

Galileo discovers the law of the pendulum observing

                      the saccharine swinging of those lovers

violently united & half consumed by the fog

believing the very foolish that Love by tooth & nail

                         will end up glowing in Technicolor

& this at the same m² / at the same time

in which the North Pole & the South Pole

the thesis & antithesis of the world

           meet

like 1 white-hot meteor & 1 UFO in distress

& inexplicably they greet each other:

I'm the 1 who embossed on the back of his denim jacket

the sentence: The nucleus of my solar system is Adventure

I call myself that but I like them to say *The Protoplasm Kid*

You're the 1 who bites his nails while leafing through the crime section

his fingers lost in the stiffness of the news page

                    but

is it the news /

          those who report it /

                    those who read it like 1 necessary drug?

who Sherlock Holmes are the assassins?

Given the circumstances you don't even trust your own eyes

what caliber of struggles pursuits disputes

                    are hidden under the roughest cloth

the fearful climb trees

the more agile prefer to walk around pointing

to the exact moment the atmosphere thins to the limit of endurance

& the airplanes start falling like 1 scene from a silent movie

where the arms of the dying spin like propeller blades

without explaining why the horizon is slobbered with fire

Although the sky—apparently—looks sober & clear

like 1 irreconcilable enemy of the Plastic Arts

& almost nobody notices the little lunatic who kisses licks bites his handless watch

while asking *Will the earth be getting colder*

          won't we be going out of orbit???

certain that in 1 such case even Jerry Lewis would sincerely weep

A poem is occurring every moment
        for example
that fluttering of mute flies
        over 1 package nobody manages to decipher
how much of it is trash & how much miracle
        for example those schoolgirls with their books tight against
          their chests
that turn the head of 1 gray-haired man with crooked glasses
while the breeze—lubricous—plays beneath their miniskirts
                For example
Laurel & Hardy who take their siestas
        dreaming the same mischief
where cake wants to serve as makeup
& 2 feet are foolish enough to enter where only 1 foot fits
          for example
the 1 who just yesterday—disguised as a woman—escaped from the psychiatric clinic
& doesn't get tired of standing on his hands & runs like 1 mad kangaroo
                  wondering about the meaning of life
about some antiseptic ointment to erase his inner bruises
                the scars from the insulin & electroshocks
while he sings in ballad form that line of Guido Cavalcanti
        Now that I can never hope to return

for example

that redheaded boy who dips his feet in the water of the fountain

& feels like Huckleberry Finn traveling on 1 tree-trunk raft

/ in the middle of the Mississippi /

or 1 bearded clochard filling his lungs with Turkish tobacco

on the banks of the Seine

seeing his name written on the water: *Lord XYZ*

while reality sails on like 1 loud & tossing steamboat

because he knows that life can kill & resurrect him

at any instant

—in 1 time & 1 place

where neither Euclid nor his stuttering geometry count—

& the immediacy the difficulty of the days running by

are seen represented by any guy who screams Help!

& dials the 911 of his consciousness

to find out what brand of life or garbage it suits him to kiss

to spit out or to look at in horror

any guy who screams or tries to & can't

while astonishment is painted (as if with burnt wax)

on his stony retired workman's face

that seems & in what a way

like a time bomb

At times / in the rush when 1 second vomits & turns white
everything is tragic / even happiness / whichever 1 you want /
Aeschylus & Harold Lloyd playing chess with beer bottle caps
but without knowing how the heck to make their creative leisure rise
        to the level of 1 earthquake that would truly wipe the slate clean
When Chaos appears all-powerful even bestial
                                        (bull-faced & faggot-voiced)
when it goes without saying that he's economically screwed
                        (You / Me / Us)
not to mention the *homemade* neurosis & anemia

& what's the use then what's the use of
                the hurricane the raffling off of things
                                that strip & invade you like amoebas
what's the use if you don't understand why overpopulation
        why abortions
                1 pregnant woman smiles at you /
if you don't capiche whether it's from desperation or from joy
that she pats her belly like Piero della Francesca's Madonna of Childbirth
if you only manage to stammer to dilate your eyes
when the pickpocket's capable hand goes to work
        / that disciple of 7-armed Shiva: God of masturbation

& the finely crafted assault /

if you only manage to gulp & make faces

when that character from Ionesco—perhaps obsessed with the bald soprano—

asks you the first chance he gets: are you sexual political

                    fundamentally satisfied?

& what's the use of getting to know the dew the gardenia expels

              in the misty dawn

as much by the sweat of your brow as the palm of your hand

as the pelvis—delicious—of the girl

that's the relief of your map

               & the compass that keeps your territory standing

what's the use if there are lives that are cars with no engines

           desperately honking their horns

              without being able to go

the life of the 1 who cures his Saturday hangover by rinsing his eyes

              at the edges of fountains

that of the high-class lady with her Chantilly cream & candy-cane hairdo

& her intolerable little voice when she says *I smoke my own*

          that whole race of sanctimonious reactionaries

who feel offended

    by the every day more frequent contact with the riff-raff

        between the soot & the sullen sun of the cities

& the life of that vagabond (the 1 word has it isn't missing)

whose lucidity is shattered / without his bicycle

    having chased any light in the Sierra Tarahumara

like his homonym Antonin Artaud

the life of the 1 who thinks too much to kiss 1 flower

            to light 1 cigarette

to say to his beloved: let's go to 1 hotel / let's blow up the moon's

    potato-white face

that of the scatterbrained bureaucrat / who screws up & more than 1 or 2 times

the 1 who'll have the same soap-opera face

      —feeling sorry for itself—

the next time he passes by here

the life of the ex–May Queen in the days of Hiroshima

    & the now neurotic grandmother of mongoloid triplets

that of the teenager penniless & up for anything

    & with hips that would have strangled the pulse

of Oscar Wilde

that of the fop who says the park

       is like the flowering liver of the city

while prancing on the tips of his toes

       around some woman who hasn't even told him her name

that of so many who have bathed 5 / 6 times

       in the black waters of failure

& not by choice (so they say)

not like those who gobble up—between smiles—1 meringue tart

       in no way like that

& that's what you always say (You / Me / Us)

while slowly buttoning up your raincoat

       —your body & your psychological defenses—

& going out for 1 walk—that will be more than 1—

       in the rain

         inside & out

       in the rain

& all because you need to you're desperate to let go & cry openly

with nobody & nothing to interrupt you

not even those chicks in hot pants

       glimmering with their bronze thighs

& clinging to the golden lampposts

& you're not the only 1 who claims to be the only passenger

> on his schizophrenic submarine

while walking (like some lunatic) with 1 burnt-out cigarette in your mouth

& the rain drenching you grotesquely

> from the top of your head to the point of your chin

Of course you're not the only 1

before whom the rusty umbrella of life

> doesn't want to spread its wings

you're not the only 1 to whom the world seems

—in moments of pessimism—

1 ghetto without bridges or streets

& also sometimes you totter & cloud over

you scratch your nose & the scab of remembrance

> Existence takes the form of 1 cop

who runs his state-of-the-art billy club down the length of your face

& you still ask: What's up my big bad wolf?

> How's repression doing?

while the marijuana bushes

planted like carrots in the subsoil of your mind tremble

& your heart is 1 crowded neighborhood

with the gutters & the roof falling down
from sheer terror
from sheer terror

Nevertheless oxygen & the regular rotation of the stars survive
September winks at us
& it's best if each of us clings to the waist of his most beloved
1 honey-colored cocker spaniel remains sunk in deep sleep
while 1 miserable fly uses his nose as 1 sofa bed
scraps rinds papers
fly about entangled in the pant cuffs of the wind
that today could shred 1 flower
                    then pummel it into the ground
but tomorrow /
            goodbye carbon dioxide /
apoplexy shitty luck Goodbye
Explain to your occasional lover
            that even 1 failed erection
is part of the process

this / & the fucking awesome vermilion of the twilight
& the flight of thrushes that for 1 instant blackens the air
& the spark of life that ruffles your chest hair
in decisive epochs
& with every appearance of becoming Epic History

Explain that to your occasional lover
        clear it up for yourself

that life is still your poetry workshop
& hopefully you'll electrify the power of your inner storm
as well as the girl with the agility of 1 sailboat
whom you've chosen as the partner of your next escapades
        that the love or the madness that most closely approximates it
                inhabit you / lighten your step
that it brighten the twinkle in your eye
        Hopefully / hopefully

The fragments the splinters from a while ago
        become in hands like Houdini's

1 scream as solid & real

as 1 breast or 1 apple

or 1 desire that turns all bodies into 1 transparent prism

The apparently static & fleeting

turns out to be 1 very important piece on the board:

behind 1 simple street photographer

                  once lived 1 Ernesto Che Guevara

& he seemed incapable of the smallest exertion

not to mention of ethical feats

The apparently static & fleeting

        turns out to be 1 very important piece on the board:

the spirit & the valor that accompany you

                 when you roam the endless avenues

remembering the poems the skin of Sappho

bathed in moonlight

when you run your hand over your face

     at the moment in which you're 1 rainbow

scratched out by the sun & the 4 o'clock drizzle

when you inscribe the poetic artifacts of this century's end
on the tree's naked trunk:

> I love you to bits
> Tú me enciendes
> You turn me on
> How can this be
> so beautiful?

—burning with faith
                & between swells of pleasure—
When you see in this the instinct of the struggle for existence
        that made Rosa Luxemburg euphoric
the living application of the heretic Wilhelm Reich's favorite theorem:
1 body is taught to read & write next to another body
        & thus the University of Tenderness is founded

when you learn to say No
        with the energy of 1 black belt in karate
or to say Yes / with the certainty

that soon the stars will have 1 color
that after enough time has passed we'll understand

The apparently static & fleeting
                threatens to burn up & with kisses
the hour when the great political rebellions seem buried
(so say the bourgeois economists from their antiaircraft introspections)

But 1 still sees life
                as deserving 1 handmade tattoo
even though right now it's posing for some invisible photographer
                that could be the burning climate itself

Even though right now it would only seem
                that Beauty is emotively radicalized
like multicolored T-shirts that say: *kiss me*
                from the most erogenous part of their torsos

like 2 brats (rumored to be hippies or anarchists)
                who promise to meet
                at that hour / at that sunset

in the Ray Bradbury Port of the channels of Mars

/ No matter what

        right there /

Under 1 sky that van Gogh would give thanks for in 6 languages /

& what whiteness will you add to this whiteness

        what spirit / what valor?

In all his poems, Santiago uses the numeral "1" in place of the impersonal pronoun ("one") and the indefinite article ("a" or "an"). In Spanish, the numeral "1" is spoken in the same way as the impersonal pronoun ("uno") and the indefinite article ("un" or "una"). We have preserved the numeral as often as possible without distorting the meaning of the poem and have substituted the indefinite article only when necessary.

The translators would like to thank Ammiel Alcalay, Zoe Azulay, Joshua Beckman, Nicole Caso, Juan Cristóbal Cerrillo, Andrew Dieck, Emma Friedland, Tomas Graman, José Montelongo, Mariano Paniello, Phil Pardi, Geoff Sanborn, Juan Villoro, and Mowgli Zendejas for their generous insight and assistance.